10 Tips for: Increasing Your Writing Speed

Seven Apps to Gamify Your Writing Sessions

Does Your Academia Fiction Make the Grade across the Pond?

Why Fact-Checking Can Make Your Fiction Stronger, and How to Find the Right People for the Job

Finding Light amid Dark Genres

No More Nine-to-Five

From Detective Inspector Declan Walsh to Doctor Who, Tony Lee's Career Has Been Anything But Ordinary—Even for an Author

INDIE AUTHOR MAGAZINE

PLOT POINTS

Issue 41

STORYTELLER
OPERATING SYSTEM

NOTION FOR AUTHORS

LEARN:

The PARA Method for Writers
Building Your Story Bible
Setting up Books and Series
Task Management for Writing
Task Management for Editing, ARCs, and Betas
Collaborating in Notion
Incorporating Other Apps into Notion
Automating Workflows
And More!

SIGN UP: INDIEAUTHORTRAINING.COM

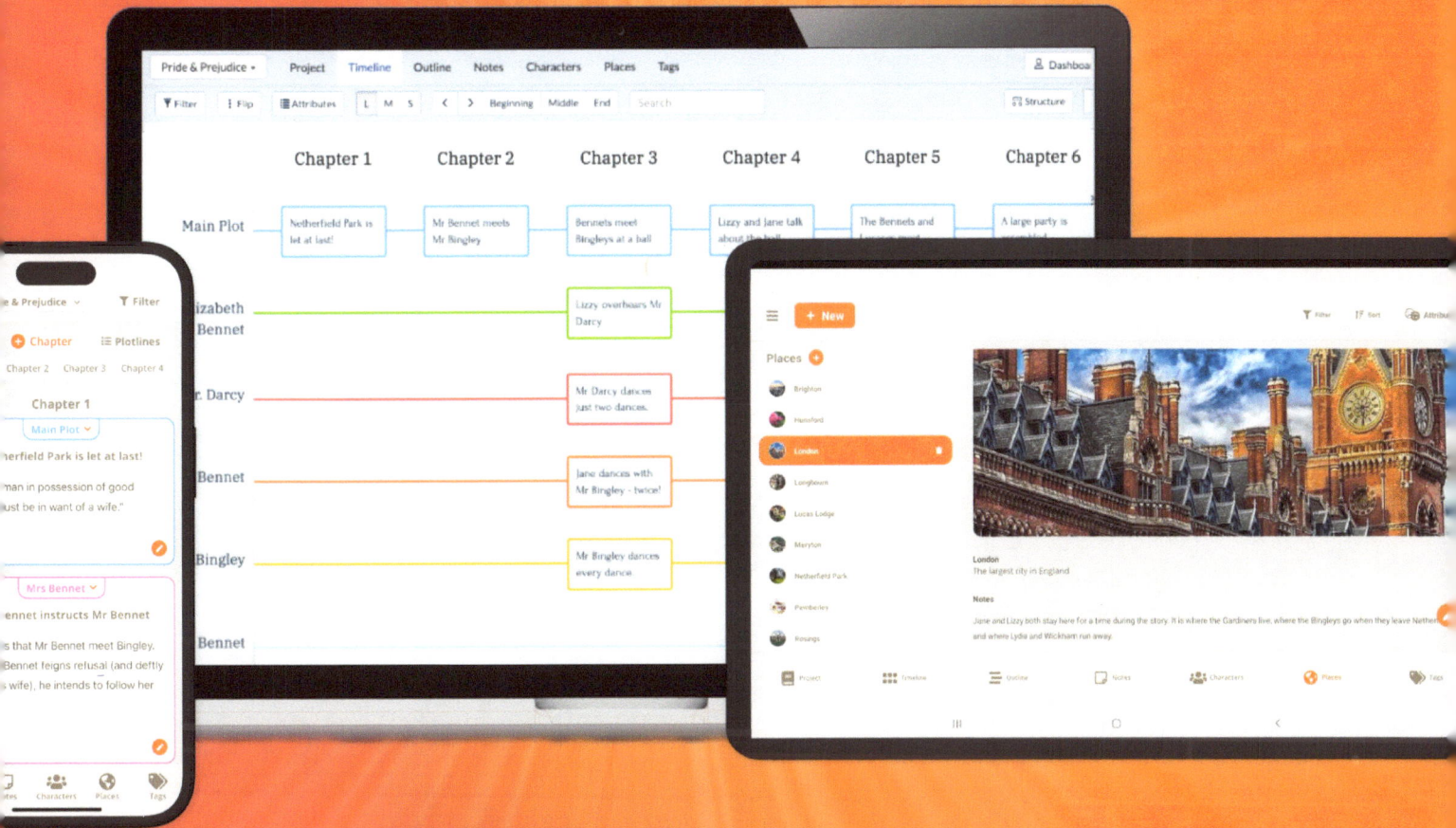

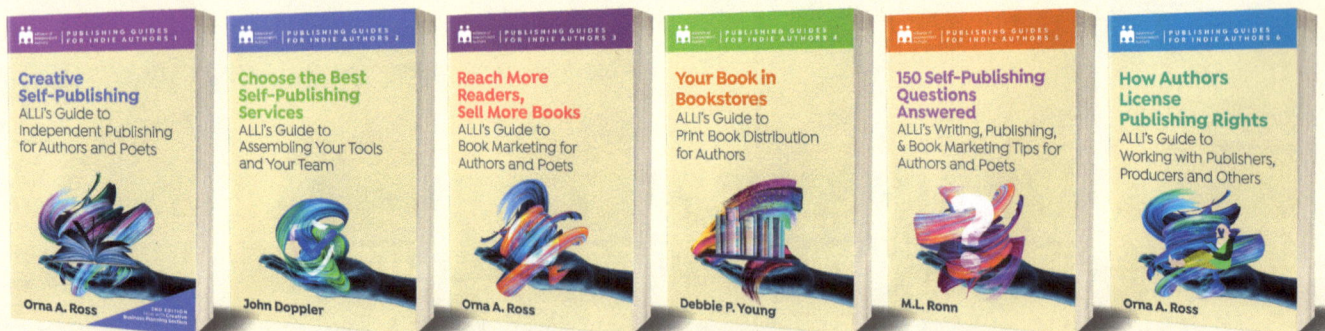

"I joined while having a crisis with Amazon KDP... The Alliance is a beacon of light. I recommend that all indie authors join...
Susan Marshall

"The Alliance is about standing together.
Joanna Penn

"It's the good stuff, all on one place.
Richard Wright

"ALLi has helped me in myriad ways: discounts on services, vetting providers, charting a course to sales success. But more than anything it's a community of friendly, knowledgeable, helpful people."
Beth Duke

See hundreds more testimonials at:
AllianceIndependentAuthors.org/testimonials

IAM
PLOT POINTS

Authorpreneurs in Action

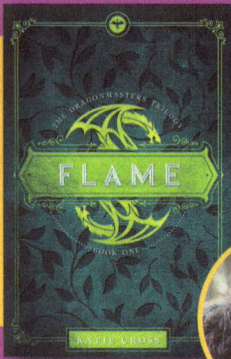

"I love Lulu! They've been a fantastic distributor of my paperbacks and an excellent partner as I dive into direct sales. They integrate so smoothly with my personal Shopify store, and their customer support has been top notch."

Katie Cross, katiecrossbooks.com

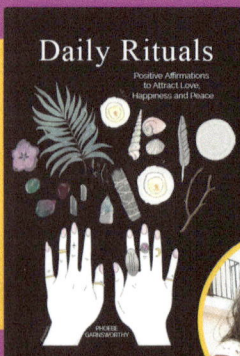

"Having my own store has given me the freedom to look at my creativity as a profitable business and lifelong career."

Phoebe Garnsworthy, phoebegarnsworthy.com

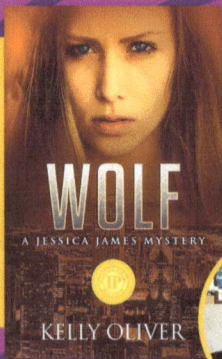

"Lulu has a super handy integration with Shopify. Lulu makes it so easy to sell paperbacks directly to readers."

Kelly Oliver, kellyoliverbooks.com

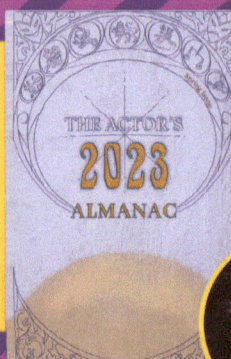

"My experience with Lulu Direct has been more convenient and simple than I anticipated or thought possible. I simply publish, take a step back and allow the well-oiled machine to run itself. Most grateful!"

Molly McGivern, theactorsalmanac.com

INDIE
AUTHOR MAGAZINE

EDITORIAL

Publisher | Chelle Honiker

Editor in Chief | Nicole Schroeder

Creative Director | Alice Briggs

Partner Relationship Manager | Elaine Bateman

ADVERTISING & MARKETING

Inquiries
Ads@AtheniaCreative.com

Information
Partner.IndieAuthorMagazine.com

CONTRIBUTORS

Angela Archer, Elaine Bateman, Bradley Charbonneau, Jackie Dana, Heather Clement Davis, Jamie Davis, Laurel Decher, Gill Fernley, Jen B. Green, Marion Hermannsen, Jenn Lessmann, Megan Linski-Fox, Angie Martin, Merri Maywether, Kevin McLaughlin, Jenn Mitchell, Tanya Nellestein, Susan Odev, Eryka Parker, Tiffany Robinson, Robyn Sarty, Joe Solari, David Viergutz

SUBSCRIPTIONS
https://indieauthormagazine.com/subscribe/

HOW TO READ
https://indieauthormagazine.com/how-to-read/

WHEN WRITING MEANS BUSINESS
IndieAuthorMagazine.com

Athenia Creative | 6820 Apus Dr., Sparks, NV, 89436 USA | 775.298.1925

ISSN 2768-7880 (online)–ISSN 2768-7872 (print)

THE NEW WAY FOR READERS TO FIND AUTHORS SELLING DIRECT

DIRECT2READERS

A unique directory where you can connect directly with your fans and keep all your hard-earned profits.

💡 Innovative Recommendation Engine: Our natural language recommendation engine helps readers discover books based on their preferences. Say goodbye to clunky categories!

📈 New Market Access: Gain exposure to a new segment of avid readers, all hungry for fresh indie voices.

💵 Zero Commissions: You read it right! We don't take a cut. Your profits are yours to keep.

🚀 Boost Your Sales: Benefit from our advanced marketing and influencer channels designed to supercharge your direct sales.

🌐 **Register Now**
Direct2Readers.com

From the
EDITOR IN CHIEF

We dedicate a lot of space in our issues each month to the challenges we face as publishers. Most are business related and depend somewhat on your experience level. Fledgling authors may care more about which email service provider to use than those who've already spread their wings, who in turn are looking for advice on translations or programs that can automate those more mundane to-dos. But no matter how long you've been working in the industry, writing never stops posing its own challenges.

I've been working on one manuscript for the past few months, another for a few months longer than that. Both are taking far longer to write than I originally expected—something another author friend, who has published several more books than me, has shared she's facing with her own projects. No matter how quickly you write, most of us dream of writing faster and publishing more.

And speed is far from the only obstacle we all recognize.

Whether it's book 3 or 33, we've all had projects where the plot just won't align, the research needed is more demanding, or the words won't appear on the page fast enough. Sometimes stories weigh on us more than we'd like when we close our laptops for the day. Sometimes they become so complicated, the blurbs that sum them up take a whole day's writing time to craft. Despite the countless ways we choose to publish, each of our businesses was built on books and the universal challenges we've faced writing them.

This issue is as much about celebrating those challenges as it is acknowledging them. At every stage, writing is what unites us, along with all the challenges, frustrations, and triumphs that come with it. I hope this month's articles will remind you of that—and give you some helpful tips along the way.

Nicole Schroeder
Editor in Chief
Indie Author Magazine

Nicole Schroeder is a storyteller at heart. As the editor in chief of Indie Author Magazine, she brings nearly a decade of journalism and editorial experience to the publication, delighting in any opportunity to tell true stories and help others do the same. She holds a bachelor's degree from the Missouri School of Journalism and minors in English and Spanish. Her previous work includes editorial roles at local publications, and she's helped edit and produce numerous fiction and nonfiction books, including a Holocaust survivor's memoir, alongside independent publishers. Her own creative writing has been published in national literary magazines. When she's not at her writing desk, Nicole is usually in the saddle, cuddling her guinea pigs, or spending time with family. She loves any excuse to talk about Marvel movies and considers National Novel Writing Month its own holiday.

ALLI EXCLUSIVE
The Art of the Blurb

Writing a compelling book sales description—also known as a blurb—is a critical skill for any author, and one that taps into a different set of writing skills than those used to create the book itself. A well-crafted blurb can significantly impact a book's sales since it, along with the title and the cover, is one of the first elements potential readers will encounter.

FOR BEGINNING AUTHORS

Focus on the Main Conflict or Theme

It's essential to understand that a book blurb is not a summary but a marketing tool. The primary goal is to intrigue potential readers and compel them to purchase your book.

Identify the main conflict or central theme of your book. For fiction, this might involve the protagonist's primary struggle or the overarching mystery. Avoid detailing every character or subplot; instead, concentrate on what makes your book unique. For nonfiction, emphasize the problem your book addresses and the solution it provides. Consider using bullet points to outline the key benefits or features of your book. This format can make it easier for readers to grasp what they will gain from reading your book.

Make sure the blurb is clear, concise, and directly addresses the reader's interests or needs.

Keep It Concise

Begin with a short, compelling hook. If you had only ten seconds to pitch your book, what would you say? This "elevator pitch" helps you distill your book's essence into a few captivating sentences. Aim for clarity and brevity, ensuring that every word counts; according to Ben Cameron of Cameron Marketing and Publicity, blurbs can be "the most important 100 words you'll ever write."

Use Engaging Language

Use vivid and emotive language to evoke curiosity and excitement. Read the blurbs of popular books in your genre to gain inspiration and to educate yourself about what works well. The goal is to create an emotional connection that makes readers eager to delve into your story.

FOR EMERGING AUTHORS

Highlight Unique Selling Points

As an emerging author, you already have a book or two under your belt. Leverage this experience by highlighting what sets your book apart. Mention awards, notable reviews, or previous successes to build credibility. If you have a specific niche or unique perspective, mention this in your blurb.

Provide Social Proof

Incorporate quotes from well-known reviewers, other authors, or industry professionals. Ensure these endorsements are relevant and come from respected sources. Avoid generic praise; instead, choose quotes that specifically highlight the strengths of your book. And of course, never pull content from a review in a way that doesn't reflect the reviewer's intent; no reviewer will appreciate you excerpting their quote "This is a great big mess of a book" as "This is a great … book."

FOR EXPERIENCED AUTHORS

Continue Refining

It's crucial to periodically revisit your blurbs. Market trends and reader preferences can change, so updating your blurb to reflect current tastes can keep your books competitive. Making even incremental refinements to your blurb can result in increased positive attention from potential readers.

Experienced authors can benefit from applying more sophisticated marketing techniques in their blurbs. Understand the psychology of persuasion to craft a blurb that not only informs but also convinces readers to buy. This might involve creating a sense of urgency, tapping into readers' emotions, or posing thought-provoking questions.

Experiment with Different Formats

You might start with a provocative question or a dramatic statement that captures the essence of your book. Another approach could be to focus on the book's atmosphere or the unique voice of the narrator. Tailor your format to best suit the genre and tone of your book.

Leverage Your Author Brand

As an established author, you have a brand that readers recognize. Use this to your advantage by ensuring your blurb reflects both your unique voice and style and provides consistency across your books.

GENERAL TIPS FOR ALL AUTHORS

Proofread Meticulously

Regardless of your experience level, always proofread your blurb multiple times. Typos and grammatical errors undermine your professionalism and deter potential readers. Engage a fellow writer to read it with a fresh pair of eyes; it's a request that's easy for others to accommodate because blurbs are so short.

Seek Feedback

Readers in your genre can provide vital input to help you fine-tune your message, perhaps identifying aspects of your blurb that can be emphasized or deemphasized to maximize its appeal to your target audience. Solicit input from your followers on social media or via your newsletter.

Test and Iterate

Test different versions of your blurb—different hooks, descriptions, and formats—to see which one performs best. Pay attention to reader feedback and sales data to determine what resonates most with your audience.

Writing an effective book blurb is a skill that evolves with practice and experience. By continuously refining your approach, you can create compelling blurbs that attract readers and boost your book sales. ■

Matty Dalrymple, ALLi Campaigns Manager

For more information, check out these two articles in ALLi's library of resources:

- https://selfpublishingadvice.org/book-blurbs-2
- https://selfpublishingadvice.org/a-new-book-blurb-could-revolutionize-your-sales

Matty Dalrymple, ALLi Campaigns Manager

The Alliance of Independent Authors (ALLi) is a global membership association for self-publishing authors. A non-profit, our mission is ethics and excellence in self-publishing. Everyone on our team is a working indie author and we offer advice and advocacy for self-publishing authors within the literary, publishing and creative industries around the world. www.allianceindependentauthors.org

Dear Indie Annie,

I keep hearing that I need to niche down into a genre to build a solid author brand, but I love writing multiple. Is it possible in our industry to build my brand around me and write what I want to write?

Genre Wanderer

Dear Genre Wanderer,

My precious Wanderer, I feel your pain. Being fenced into one genre simply won't do! That's like being told you can only sip one type of tea for the rest of your life. Earl Grey today, Earl Grey tomorrow, Earl Grey until you grow dowdy and gray yourself? Perish the thought! (Especially as I can't abide Earl Grey. Give me a robust Darjeeling any day.)

Although the business side of your head will shriek marketing at you, and brands strive for cohesion, routine, and expectation, we artists crave variety! What is life without the delightful surprise of occasionally swapping your breakfast builder's brew for a dreamy chamomile? The palate revels in exploration.

So rather than confining your flourishing author flower to one restrictive genre garden, consider instead how your personal brand could be like a sumptuous tea house overflowing with whimsical blends and fanciful flavors. You are the master brewmaker and tea sommelier in one.

Perhaps your Cozy Mystery tales are the homey house black tea, ever reliable and deeply comforting. But then you dazzle with poetry—a vibrant herbal infusion brimming with zest and refreshing notes. Meanwhile, your Urban Fantasy unleashes exotic spiced-masala chai that transports readers to realms of pure enchantment.

By packaging and presenting each delicious story experience as a unique speciality blend, you celebrate your versatility rather than stifling it. Devoted patrons will eagerly return to explore the ever-evolving tea leaf menu at the House of Your Imagination.

This approach has served many prolific authors well. Neil Gaiman sips from nearly every genre pot: Mythic Fantasy (*Stardust*), Sci-Fi (*The Sandman*), children's fables (*Coraline*), and

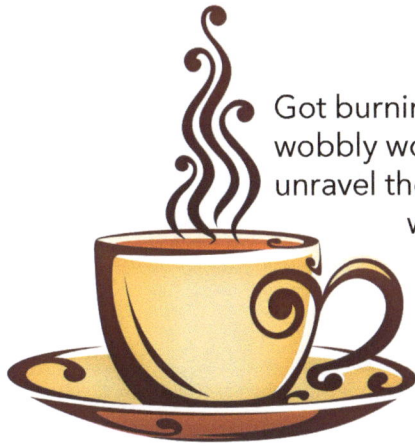

Got burning questions about the wibbly-wobbly world of indie authoring? Eager to unravel the mysteries of publishing, writing woes, or anything in between? Give your quizzical quills a whirl and shoot your musings over to indieannie@ indieauthormagazine.com. Your inky quandaries are my cup of tea!

more. His signature? Incomparable story-telling and world-building.

Or look to Maya Angelou, who master-fully vacillated between memoir (*I Know Why the Caged Bird Sings*), poetry (*Just Give Me a Cool Drink of Water 'fore I Diiie*), plays, jour-nalism, and more. Her truest devotion was to evoking the human experience.

Even the master himself, Stephen King, while eternally brewing Horror, has concocted forays into Supernatural Fiction (*The Green Mile*), Suspense (*Misery*), Speculative Sci-Fi (*Under the Dome*), and Literary Fiction's darkest Earl Greys.

Despite their variety, each of these writers has a unique voice that tells the reader that it is their glorious work, and their fans can't get enough.

Yes, some people think chamomile tastes like grass and Earl Grey like a lady's boudoir, but you can never satisfy all tastes. I believe there are even people who don't drink tea at all. Scandalous!

The decision you have to make, my dear, is how you want to package your work. Gaiman, Angelou, and King confidently use one name on every venture. J. K. Rowling, queen of the Harry Potter world, prefers to be Robert

Galbraith for her Cormoran Strike books. Having multiple pen names is not uncommon, especially for books in different genres. If that helps with the brand of those titles, then use a pseudonym. If your Sci-Fi books may adversely damage the sales of your Steamy Romances, then publish under a different name. Other-wise, if all your amazing stories have a golden thread, stand proud and publish as Genre Wanderer. The trick, my dear, is to let your audience know what treats they can expect. Like the ritual of the Japanese tea ceremony, it is important to prepare yourself and your guests for the delights that lie ahead, whether they will explore one taste or many flavors.

Chin up, my darling! If one flavor is not for you, niche not into tidy genres but into an extravagant author brand tailored especially for the fearless, eclectic literary wanderer in you. There's no novel, memoir, or pantoum you can't stir to perfection. Now brew up and serve the world something splendid!

Happy writing,
Indie Annie
X

10 TIPS FOR
INCREASING YOUR WRITING SPEED

Ask a group of authors what they'd change about their writing routine, and most are likely to say, "I wish I could write faster and publish more." For many of us, there never seem to be enough hours in the day to reach the word counts we aspire to, but that doesn't mean we should lay down our pens or close the lids of our laptops and give up.

Like most things in life, the more you work at increasing your writing speed, the easier it will be to see progress. Fortunately, for authors looking to up their word counts, there are as many tricks and tools for increasing your writing speed as there are cute cat videos on YouTube. While the following list is far from exhaustive, it does offer a variety of methods many authors have found helpful for increasing their daily word counts and finishing that first draft faster.

1. ORGANIZE TO ENERGIZE

Being prepared works for the Boy Scouts, and it can work for you too. Try defining specific writing targets, like word counts or the number of chapters, to accomplish each day. Having clear objectives can keep you focused and on track.

Before beginning a new project, creating an outline can prevent you from getting stuck and help you move quickly from one scene to the next. If you find outlining too restrictive, try creating a list of major moments that will occur throughout your story or jot down a quick paragraph or two that captures your thoughts for each chapter so that when you reach that spot later, you're not left staring at a blank page.

Those who favor complete "pantsing" may want to consider techniques like the one used by Ernest Hemingway, who stopped his writing sessions mid-sentence so he knew exactly where to start his next session. Whether a pantser or a planner, batch writing-related tasks like brainstorming, outlining, and editing. Focusing on one task at a time can be more efficient, especially so you're not having to make creative decisions while in a business mindset.

② GET ZEN BEFORE PICKING UP YOUR PEN

Working in a peaceful writing space can put you in the frame of mind to write like the wind. Set up a comfortable and distraction-free environment. Having a dedicated space tailored to your optimal writing mood can help you get into the writing mindset more quickly and keep you there longer. Include items that make you feel calm and productive, such as fuzzy slippers, a warm blanket, scented candles, or your favorite mug.

Try writing at the same time every day to condition your mind to expect writing time, making it easier to start and maintain momentum. During this time, minimize interruptions by turning off notifications, blocking distracting websites, and letting others know you're unavailable.

③ MAKE WRITING A CHALLENGE

When writing is fun, it's easy to level up, so why not try sprints for the win? Set a timer for fifteen to thirty minutes and write as much as you can without stopping. Whether you do this on your own or as part of a group, sprints can be a great way to hone your physical and mental writing muscles and increase your speed. You could even gamify your writing by using an app like the Most Dangerous Writing App (https://www.squibler.io/dangerous-writing-prompt-app), which deletes your writing if you don't work fast enough, or Written? Kitten! (https://writtenkitten.co), which rewards you with cute kitty pictures for meeting your word goals.

Use tools like word count trackers or writing apps to monitor your daily word count with the goal of beating your previous day's words each day. Seeing your accomplishments can motivate you to keep writing quickly.

Engaging in writing challenges like National Novel Writing Month (NaNoWriMo) is a great way to push yourself to write more in a short period.

Pro Tip: When participating in group activities like sprints, make sure to agree on the rules beforehand. Having everyone on the same page and knowing what to expect from the session keeps the group productive yet fun.

④ KEEP THE WORD TRAIN ROLLING

When the goal is speed, it's best to avoid habits that derail your ability to move forward in your story. Consider starting your session with a few minutes of freewriting to clear your mind and get into the flow.

Embracing imperfection can help you focus on getting words down faster rather than crafting perfect sentences. You can always edit later, but you can't edit a blank page. The key is to keep the momentum going. If you find yourself stuck on a detail, use a placeholder such as "[description here]" and move on. Also limit research during writing time—instead, make notes on what needs further investigation and research later.

Set deadlines. Even self-imposed deadlines can create a sense of urgency and motivate you to write faster.

Pro Tip: In his book *Writing into the Dark*, author Dean Wesley Smith describes a looping technique that helps writers reinforce the habit of not editing or re-reading while getting through their first draft. If you get stuck, he writes, go back a few hundred words and revise or rewrite those paragraphs. Then, keep writing. He also suggests writing out of order as inspiration strikes and outlining chapters after you finish them to spot patterns or plot threads in your writing.

(5) EMBRACE TECHNOLOGY TO SCALE YOUR SPEED

Scrivener, Ulysses, and even basic word processors often have minimalistic modes to help you stay focused and organized. Many software programs also offer tools like word count trackers, timers, and reviews of your manuscripts that can help you improve your writing and track writing speed.

If you find typing slower than speaking, then why not try your hand, or rather your voice, at dictation to up your word count? Using speech-to-text software like Dragon Dictation can help you get your ideas down quickly, with only minimal edits required to correct transcription issues. Try dictating your first draft, then go back and edit for clarity and style. This separation can speed up the drafting process.

Pro Tip: While many authors shy away from letting AI do their actual writing, it can also be a useful tool for increasing writing speed. Most AI programs use natural language processing to help it understand human language, which means it can be useful for helping you find the right word or phrasing, brainstorming when you're stuck, and even translating your work.

(6) WRITE WHEN IT FEELS RIGHT

Not everyone writes in the same way, at the same time of day, or for the same amount of time. Identify when you're most creative and focused during the day and schedule your writing sessions during these times. Try several locations, public and private, to get a feel for the spaces, noise levels, and levels of interaction with others that allow you to work your best.

Consider keeping a log of your word counts in a variety of writing environments. Keeping track of times, moods, and places when you're least or most productive can provide valuable insight and clue you into what to seek out or avoid when trying to increase your productivity.

(7) CREATE A WRITING PLAYLIST

Some writers find that listening to certain music or ambient sounds can help them focus and write faster. Try asking other writers what they listen to when writing, or check out playlists on YouTube and your favorite go-to music apps.

You can even bring your audience in on the fun. Consider asking existing or potential readers for their suggestions. Not only is this a great way to engage with your audience, but it might even encourage you to write faster so you can grow your reader list.

(8) JOIN A WRITING GROUP

Try getting social for success. Writing groups are a great place for sharing tips and techniques, learning new processes, and hearing what is and isn't working for others with goals similar to your own. Search Facebook, Discord, or other social media for groups that focus on sprints or other activities that help increase your output.

Pro Tip: When choosing a writing group, be sure they mesh well with you and your writing so they can help you reach your author goals. It's important that you get along with them, but you'll also need them to fit with your writing style and commitment level like a favorite pair of comfy pants.

---

(9) HEAD BACK TO CLASS

If you've tried increasing your writing speed on your own but still haven't found the success you've been hoping for, consider signing up for a class, course, or coaching sessions with fellow authors. They're great for learning new habits, methods, and techniques that can increase your productivity. A simple web search will turn up tons of options, but also consider getting recommendations from professional organizations, such as the Alliance of Independent Authors, or fellow authors you trust. Or check out IAM's sister site, Indie Author Training (https://indieauthortraining.com), which offers a library of courses and tech webinars from vetted, knowledgeable experts across the industry.

---

(10) DON'T BE AFRAID TO PIVOT

Set aside time regularly to review your writing process, and identify areas where you can improve efficiency. Adjust your approach based on what works best for you. It's okay to stop doing things that aren't providing results in order to make room for new things that might. When it comes to increasing your writing speed, there is no single path to success. Try experimenting with these and other strategies until you find the combination that works best for you. ■

Jenn Mitchell

Jenn Mitchell

Jenn Mitchell writes Urban Fantasy and Weird West, as well as culinary cozy mysteries under the pen name, J Lee Mitchell. She writes, cooks, and gardens in the heart of South Central Pennsylvania's Amish Country. When she's not doing these things, she dreams of training llama riding ninjas.

She enjoys traveling, quilting, hoarding cookbooks, Sanntangling, and spending time with the World's most patient and loving significant other.

No More Nine-to-Five

FROM DETECTIVE INSPECTOR DECLAN WALSH TO DOCTOR WHO, TONY LEE'S CAREER HAS BEEN ANYTHING BUT ORDINARY—EVEN FOR AN AUTHOR

For thirty-plus years, multi-modal writer Tony Lee has been no stranger to the industry. He started by writing game reviews for a British magazine at sixteen years old, and now, his name is associated with successful franchises such as *Doctor Who*, *Starship Troopers*, DC Comics, Marvel Comics, and Star Trek. With over 170 million pages reads on Kindle Unlimited and five hundred thousand books sold, Tony, writing as Jack Gatland, is a veteran of the writing community. But he didn't start off as a writer. At twenty years old, he was partially paralyzed, and with nothing else to do but write, he began working on a radio comedy sketch show, which springboarded his career as a writer, where he could create without boundaries.

———— ~~ ————

Tony has been a hustler his entire life, having made the most life-changing decision of his entire career in his early thirties. That was when fellow writer Andy Briggs, known for his work in film, comics, and TV, steered him to chat with fellow author and screenwriter Barry Hutchinson about independent publishing. It was also when COVID-19 sparked a global lockdown and a dramatic shift in people's careers across industries. In the midst of 2020, Tony took it as a sign that all the things he had been doing to write

professionally—comics, film, TV, and network shows—had dried up. He had been doing school talks—then schools had closed. And in September 2020, Tony had six months' worth of money saved to give writing a good go—or else return to a nine-to-five, something he says he dreaded more than anything. "As a freelancer, you work all the hours," he says. "What terrified me about the nine-to-five is I wouldn't be writing."

He still finds it terrifying, he admits.

At this pivotal time, Tony discovered the 20BooksTo50K® group and found a lifeline. He could publish his work and get paid for it without using an agent. Tony had been writing crime dramas for TV and film that hadn't been commissioned yet, so he took them all and created a crime novel universe that he published under the pen name Jack Gatland.

That decision was in September 2020, and by November 2020, he had written his first reader magnet.

His projects, once commissioned for TV, were named *Dead Letter*, *Duality*, and *Hunter Hunted*. Under Jack Gatland, those manuscripts became the now-world-renowned Detective Inspector Declan Walsh series. The end of November 2020 saw his first book—*Letter from the Dead*—out in the world, and in January 2021, he published the second book in the series, which he titled *Murder of Angels*. By February 2023, he had published the third book. He kept the title *Hunter Hunted* for that novel—because who wouldn't? Now, the series comprises nineteen books, which makes for a total of thirty-one across Tony's entire catalog.

"When I did this, I genuinely thought this was my Band-Aid, so I could pay some bills while I waited for my real job to start," he says. "By book 4, I realized this was my real job. Now, as we talk here four years later, I've got thirty-one books out. It's become my life."

~

Tony's move into self-publishing wasn't the end of his career in comics, film, TV, and games. As the industry came back to life following the pandemic, he began writing for other mediums again alongside his novel-writing career. He still has his hands in the entertainment industry and currently has four manuscripts optioned for production.

Moving into the average writerly discussions of a not-so-average guy, Tony says his writing process involves half-plotting, half-pantsing, and at the end of a novel, he has a pair of editors who put the gloss on his story. One of his editors is a literal rocket scientist—who also happens to be his brother—and he helps Tony with the developmental side of his work. He then sends the manuscript to his final editor for a copyediting pass before handing it off to a loyal team of beta readers.

His writing speed he attributes to dictation. Tony says he likes to dictate while he walks, then uses AI to clean things up after—anything to give him back five minutes in his busy schedule, he says. He uses his time walking the dog to record on his phone, a special AI-powered recorder, or his Apple Watch. During this time, he says he's able to dictate around 2,500 words, which just need a pass through ChatGPT and his custom GPT to clean things up a bit.

Tony attributes half of his time as dedicated writing time; the rest of it he commits to the aspects of publishing beyond the words. In that 50 percent, alongside his administrative tasks, he manages to fit running a comic convention in the UK and school visits to meet readers of his best-selling children's books, which helped him earn the "*New York Times* bestseller" title. He also funds the £2,500 Caliburn Prize, a yearly grant for unpublished UK comic creators.

When asked how he manages all the multiple projects he has going on, he says his life runs on Notion, the project management software. He micromanages himself down to the minute in certain cases. But like a typical writer, he has a little bit of chaos in his life, too. "You have to get on the bike and start cycling," he says. "After a few miles, you get into the groove of how to cycle, [but] during those first few miles, you're struggling, falling off, stumbling, getting back up again." Tony says he thrives on deadlines, but he loves to watch them pass him by. And although he would like to slow down a bit, his lingering fear of the ordinary desk job gives him the energy to keep pedaling.

Tony's story is one of perseverance, with lessons for seasoned and new writers alike. Tony takes the title writer and applies it to multiple mediums across multiple industries, all with the intent of telling a damn good story. But his own story, of stumbling into writing and then declaring it the last thing he wants to let go of, is one most authors share.

Left to our own devices, writers will write, whether it be for BBC radio dramas, film, television, comics, or the independent writing community. Any onlooker will still find Tony doing what he loves—instead of making the shift from one industry to the other, however, he's doing both. Whether he's writing as Jack Gatland or *New York Times* Bestselling Author Tony Lee, the man is here to be a creative and tell stories for millions around the globe to enjoy—in whatever form they take. ∎

David Viergutz

David Viergutz

David Viergutz is a disabled Army Veteran, Law Enforcement Veteran, husband and proud father. He is an author of stories from every flavor of horror and dark fiction. One day, David's wife sat him down and gave him the confidence to start putting his imagination on paper. From then on out his creativity has no longer been stifled by self-doubt and he continues to write with a smile on his face in a dark, candle-lit room.

SOLARI SAYS

Reframe Failure as a Path to Success

Business mindset is just as important as business strategy, says Managing Director of Author Nation Joe Solari in part 3 of his quarterly series. Plenty of indie authors limit their growth by avoiding taking risks or telling themselves they won't succeed at certain publishing ventures, but Solari says failure is the biggest teacher we have—and often, it means we're one step farther along the path to success. This month, he encourages authors to embrace a paradigm shift and the idea of failure, so they can embrace new opportunities down the road.

I recently met with an old economics professor of mine who reached out to me to discuss book publishing. He finds himself in an interesting position: he has a book that he wants to publish, but he is conflicted because of his paradigm.

In his world as a University of Chicago professor, there is only one kind of publishing—academic publishing. You write a book, get peers to review it, and then find a publication of a certain "caliber."

He knows my work with authors, so we sat down to talk about a different way of publishing. A way that you understand—the indie way.

He told me that 100 percent of his students whom he teaches economics never become economists. They learn how to apply economics to the real world. I would put myself in that category. I learned a lot about economics from him and have applied it to my daily operations.

He met with me because he feels that self-publishing is the more productive path, but twenty-three years of institutional thinking and being surrounded by others with a vested interest in that thinking make it difficult for him to apply some of the best lessons he has taught about failure.

He says that there are only two types of failure: failure of imagination and failure of courage. As an outsider, it is easy for me to see how he suffers from both and limits his beliefs to those that fit within his paradigm.

I have invited him to Author Nation so he can have his paradigm shifted.

All of us stay where we are comfortable because it gives us the illusion of safety. That same comfort reinforces mindsets that limit our imagination and induce institutional fears that sap our courage. It's easy for us who have embraced indie publishing to see how a tenured professor is limiting his imagination by not embracing a publishing path that offers far more control and is better suited to reaching his ideal audience.

Rather than judge him, ask yourself, "What am I myopic about? What reality have I framed that limits my imagination?"

How are we challenging our paradigms and pushing beyond our comfort zones? Embracing new paths requires imagination and courage, and it's essential to recognize where we might be holding ourselves back.

So much of failure is a failure of courage. We live in a world where all we are shown is how easy it is and how successful others have been. This leads us to not take action—sometimes to the point of not even starting. The comparison makes us feel like we are failing when we are not.

It's easy to say that true failure is not to try at all. The other end of the spectrum is not knowing when to give up. I know from my own experience that I have tried and failed numerous times, and I have also made some failures worse by not giving up sooner when it was clear that the situation would not improve. The emotional and economic costs were substantial, impacting not just my finances but also my mental well-being and stress levels. However, despite these significant challenges, the experience and learning I gained were the big payoff.

Somewhere in between a failure to start and a failure to stop is where we find success. Each failure taught me valuable lessons about resilience, perseverance, and the importance of knowing when to pivot or abandon a course of action. These insights have proven invaluable in navigating future endeavors and making more informed decisions. I hope you, too, can benefit from what I've learned, but if you're like me, the only way you'll truly learn is by doing it. ■

Joe Solari

Joe Solari

Joe Solari is an author, entrepreneur, and consultant. Since 2016 he has been helping best-selling authors build great publishing businesses. He has worked to create tools and systems to help passionate business owners professionalize their team and operations to achieve exceptional results.

Ask the Experts

WHY FACT-CHECKING CAN MAKE YOUR FICTION STRONGER, AND HOW TO FIND THE RIGHT PEOPLE FOR THE JOB

Your manuscript is finished; you have taken your beta readers' input and made changes suggested by your agent or content editor. You are ready to set your manuscript aside until publish day, right? Well, not quite. Whether your writing is a novel, a short story, or a travel diary, it isn't just your grammar that needs to be correct.

In recent years, media discussions about fact checkers have abounded in the political arena. That is not the only place where fact checkers dwell. Even with fiction stories, readers will speak up if you write about historical events and place them in the wrong era, or if you describe an internal combustion engine incorrectly or confuse the steps in construction or repairs to an old home. You need to be certain you describe those details properly. Your editor may catch some slip-ups, but to ensure you have your facts right, it's best to find an expert on the subject or someone who is a member of a particular community. An artist may be able to explain how long it takes acrylic paint to dry or why certain materials are better to use for painting; a chef can inform you why a menu with umami, one of the five basic tastes, is important to a meal.

Reaching out to experts is even more important when you need to represent a community you don't belong to. If your travel memoir mentions traveling with a wheelchair or with oxygen, speak with real people who require help with such devices about their experiences regarding ADA-compliant access with trains, planes, and bus travel; don't make assumptions that because there are laws about travel, all transportation is now easy. If you choose a name for a character of a different ethnicity from yours, determine that the names you select fit into that demographic correctly. For example, Asian names are not interchangeable; some are specific to Korean culture while others are part of Chinese heritage. Many cultures do not require spouses to use the same last name or add extensions to the family names for the children. In many of these cases, it's impossible to truly understand experiences and situations through research alone, but sensitivity readers are an integral part of the editing process and can tell you exactly how to represent those situations in your story in order to make it feel authentic.

GOING PRO

If you decide your draft could benefit from a more specialized review, either in certain passages or for plot or character elements that occur throughout the book, subject matter experts, or SMEs, can often cut down the research you'll need to do and provide more specific feedback on your story. SME is not an official title or degree but a recognition of specific skills that may be helpful as you're revising your book. According to the job site Indeed.com, "Subject matter experts, or SMEs, are authorities in their field who can provide expertise to fill knowledge gaps on a project or within a company. Although many professionals today undergo cross-training in several areas, SMEs are in great demand because of their deep understanding of their chosen field."

SMEs often have years of formal education or training and firsthand experience within their field. As you're searching for SMEs related to a topic, look first at contacts in your community who are already recognized as successful in their field from awards they received or press notices. Do you have friends, neighbors, or relatives with unique skill sets related to your story? Then turn to books or articles in your targeted field; who is writing them? What topics and people are trending on social media that tie into the details you're researching?

You might wonder how to approach these experts, but many like to provide explanations or describe their field of expertise to someone else. Introduce yourself as an author working on a short story or novel and explain the questions you're hoping to answer. If your introductory email or phone call mentions some aspect of their writing or website that drew you in, your SME might be eager to assist. Flattery often works! And if you run into someone who is too busy to reply or is a curmudgeon, don't be discouraged; move on to others on your list.

TIPS FOR YOUR SME SEARCH

Once you have identified your SMEs, keep the following tips in mind to make sure your discussions provide the answers you need.

Know who you're talking to. Review their website, if any. Peruse any books or magazine articles written recently, and explore any online appearances such as on YouTube, Instagram, or local or national media appearances. You'll know better the questions to ask them and maybe get a few of the more obvious details cleared up before you reach out.

Prepare a list of questions for your contact. Make sure you're organized and know what you want to ask ahead of time. You may think you won't forget, but it can be easy to get sidetracked in a conversation, and there's nothing worse than hanging up the call and realizing you forgot to check the most important detail in your story.

Prepare a script that explains your reasons for reaching out to them. Phone calls work, but email may be preferred for its flexibility. If you're calling or meeting in person, suggest several options for your contact time to allow them to schedule a time convenient for them.

Be respectful. Keep the conversation short and to the point. If you can, set up a Zoom call that would define your time parameters.

Pro Tip: If you wish to record their responses, get their permission in advance. This isn't just good etiquette; depending on where you live, disclosing that you're recording a conversation may be a legal requirement.

Follow up. Be gracious and thank them for their time and knowledge, and follow up with a written response. Tell them when or where your work will be published if you can, so they can look at it or cite it later. Ask if you can reach out later, should additional clarifications be necessary. Know that you may also reach out to additional experts; you are not limited to just one.

Give credit where it's due. Beyond thanking your SME personally, it may be a nice gesture to shout them out in your book's acknowledgments. Here are some sample acknowledgments to give you an idea.

In her bestselling novel about nurses who served in the Vietnam War, *The Women*, Kristin Hannah thanked the many nurses she consulted about their experiences by name, saying in part, "You truly are an inspiration," "Thank you for taking the time to read and critique an early draft and answer questions," and "Thank you for sharing personal photographs and memories."

In her Cozy Mystery set in Puerto Rico, *Barbacoa, Bombas, and Betrayal,* author Raquel V. Reyes acknowledges the cooks of that island who inspired her and taught her local cooking traditions. She referenced specific YouTube and Instagram accounts, local cooks, and cookbooks by name.

A more formal recognition was made in the epic biography *American Prometheus: The Triumph and Tragedy of J. Robert Oppenheimer* by authors Kai Bird and Martin J. Sherwin, who acknowledged their SMEs by saying: "We are indebted to several eminent scholars who took the time to carefully read early versions of our manuscript. Jeremy Bernstein, also an Oppenheimer biographer, is an accomplished physicist and writer who did his best to correct our wrong-headed apprehensions of quantum physics."

Of course, after your interview with your SME, you might need to make changes in your manuscript to correct any deficiencies or descriptions revealed by your newly gained information. But the result will be a stronger, more believable story for your readers to devour. So, indie author, start your search. Using the tips above should make it easier. ■

Sharon Kay Dooley

Sharon Kay Dooley

Sharon Kay Dooley is a semi-retired Registered Nurse who has been a writer since her high school days. Sharon loves word games, Wordle, and puzzles. She has always been a reader and reads everything except horror and most Sci-fi. Currently, she is writing a series of children's books and an environmentally based cozy mystery series.

Since she lives in MD near the nation's capital, she keeps an eye on politics and the Washington Football Team-The Commanders. She includes among her special favorites her two children, and her grandchildren. Other likes are cooking, drinking excellent coffee, eating chocolate desserts, and walks with her rescue dog.

Seven Apps to Gamify Your Writing Sessions, and Other Author-Approved Methods for Boosting Your Word Count

No matter how much we love writing, every author knows the struggle of days when the words won't flow and our attention wants to drift to other things. Maintaining a regular writing schedule means some sessions are inherently more productive than others—but that doesn't mean you can't trick yourself into putting words down on the page anyway.

Across several categories, including education, health and fitness, and sustainability, research has shown gamification can provide at least temporary positive benefits for users who are looking to increase consistency of a behavior or productivity toward a goal. Indie author and video game journalist Grace Snoke writes that the same benefits can happen when gamifying writing. "I liken it to achievement hunting in video games," Snoke writes. "In some games, you may not know the achievements and are surprised by them when you earn them. Other games, you know the achievement and are working hard to get it, then you celebrate when you get it. With writing novels, or even short stories, there is also the achievement of writing 5,000, 10,000, or more words. And there's an even bigger sense of achievement at finishing the novel. It gives the same dopamine burst as getting an achievement in a game does."

Author Audrey Hughey agrees. She uses gamification techniques and platforms for both her fiction and nonfiction writing as a way to motivate herself through less immediately rewarding tasks. "Writing a book is often a long-haul journey where you won't see rewards until you publish and market your tail off," she writes. "Gamifying writing keeps us writing, even when our long-term rewards can seem hidden in the foggy landscape of the future."

Gamifying writing sessions is not a new concept; in fact, several platforms and sites already exist to help authors boost their daily word counts and maintain a consistent writing schedule. We've gathered a list of some of the most popular ones that are worth a try the next time you hit a slump and need to level up your productivity.

WRITING

Written? Kitten!

https://writtenkitten.co

Sometimes motivating yourself to write is as simple as having the right reward. Written? Kitten! finds suitably adorable options among Flickr's "most interesting" photos, displaying a new random photo of a kitten after every hundred words you write. The word count requirements you need to meet before the site offers a new photo can be adjusted, as can its image search parameters. Click on the link at the bottom of the site's web page and edit the URL in your browser to specify the image keyword you'd like to use instead.

The Most Dangerous Writing App

https://squibler.io/dangerous-writing-prompt-app

With several authors and writing-focused social media accounts spotlighting the app recently—searches on TikTok for the app return 70.9 million post results—the Most Dangerous Writing App has also become one of the most popular. Set your session timer and start writing, but once you start, don't stop or the app will delete your progress. Rather than a timer, you can set a session word count, and "hardcore mode" also gives users the option to blur everything they've already written. The Most Dangerous Writing App may be a terrifying prospect to some, but to others, it's the perfect way to break through writer's block ... or else.

4thewords

https://4thewords.com

Other apps gamify individual writing sessions, but 4thewords turns the writing process into a true fantasy game, with an avatar to level up, in-world quests, combat encounters, and a world map—and interacting with or unlocking any of it requires you to write. Battles against monsters are speed- or endurance-based writing challenges, and quests require you to complete a number of battles, write a certain number of words, or maintain a writing streak for a set number of days in order to earn collectibles or gear. The app has both free and paid options, with subscribers having access to additional features such as more customization options within the game and support for more than one project per account. Subscriptions cost $96 annually for Member accounts and $144 annually for Pro accounts.

Pro Tip: Hughey started using 4thewords earlier this year after she saw some friends using it. She even used the site when writing her responses to *IAM*, she admits. "I think what I enjoy most about 4thewords is the ability to get in some fun, no-pressure gaming at the same time as working on my writing projects, which are deeply important to me," she writes. "Also, my writing time is easier to guard with 4thewords because my (school-age) kids love games, too, and they understand quests and time limits. When I 'play,' they cheer me on and want me to win."

Ohwrite

https://ohwrite.co

If you're motivated more by the idea of group writing challenges, Ohwrite allows you to host writing sprints with other authors in a virtual sprint room. Users can set a timer for all participants at once and write directly in the app, and once the sprint is finished, the app will display competitors' word counts on the right side of the page. The app also tracks your writing progress over days, weeks, and months using the site, so you can view your individual statistics over time if you're sprinting consistently.

Pro Tip: Beyond apps specifically built with game mechanics, several word processors include features that can track or boost your productivity during writing sessions. Scrivener users can set a manuscript or session target word count to create a gauge at the top of the project that changes colors as they near their goals, and Atticus offers several tools for drafting books faster, including a habit tracker and built-in sprint timer.

GENERAL PRODUCTIVITY

Staying focused during writing sessions is important, but as indie authors, we juggle plenty of other non-writing responsibilities as well. If you're looking to gamify the business tasks on your list, or if you prefer more general productivity tools to keep you focused on your manuscript, here are a few additional apps to try.

Flora

https://flora.appfinca.com/en

Inspired by the Pomodoro technique, Flora is an iOS and Android app that encourages users to stay off their phone and on task with a virtual garden that flourishes the more time you spend focused. Set a timer, then set your phone aside; if you avoid leaving the Flora app during that time, you'll receive a flower, tree, or plant to add to your garden, but if you exit the focus screen before the timer goes off, your plant will die. As you complete more focus sessions, you'll be able to travel to other regions of the world and collect new plants, and if you want to up the ante, you can also put money on the line—the app will only charge you if you kill your plant, with the money going toward planting real trees in Africa, East Asia, and South America. The app also includes an in-app to-do list, tools for tracking time spent focused, and a friends list so you can run focus sessions with other app users.

Forest

https://forestapp.cc

Forest is another iOS and Android app, incredibly similar to Flora. The app is a paid app rather than a free app with in-app purchases like Flora. However, successful focus sessions in Forest reward users with coins that can be used to purchase a greater variety of trees, ambient music, and other customizations for their virtual forests, as well as to plant real trees with the organization Trees for the Future via the Real Forest tab. The app also includes features that allow you to sort trees into forests based on tags and track your focus statistics, set calendar reminders to run a focus session, and invite friends to a focus room, similar to Flora.

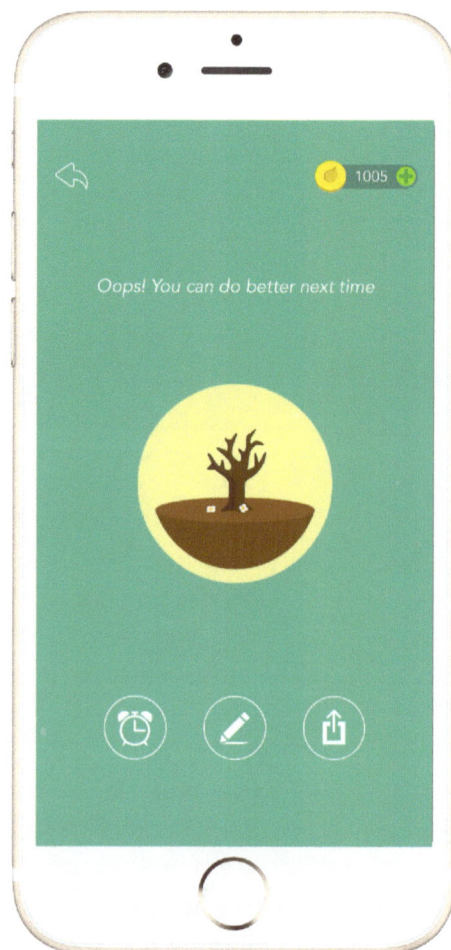

Habitica

https://habitica.com

If 4thewords turns your writing sessions into a fantasy game, Habitica does the same for your to-do list. Using role-play game mechanics, users create a character and enter their to-dos, daily tasks, habits, and rewards into the site. Checking off tasks earns you gold and experience points, but marking a negative habit or missing a daily task costs you health. As time goes on and you gain more experience, you'll have the ability to level up and select from one of four classes: healer, warrior, mage, or rogue, as well as join an adventuring party with other players. Users can also complete quests, collect pets and mounts, and join sitewide challenges to earn gold and equipment—all by checking off tasks and positive habits regularly. The app is free to use, though some customizations and quests cost gems, which are purchasable, or a paid subscription.

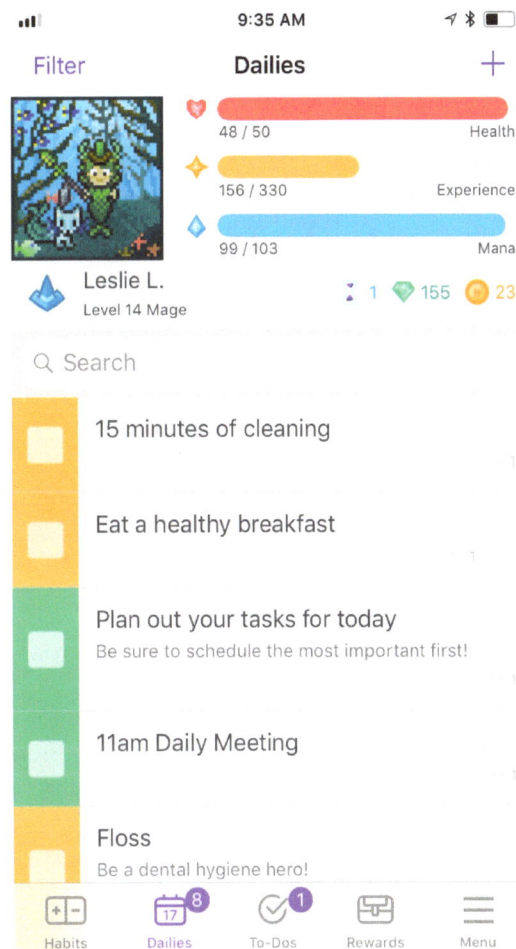

OTHER GAMIFYING METHODS

Of course, even beyond gamifying apps, there are countless ways to turn your writing sessions into fun challenges or competitions. Snoke has used several strategies for keeping herself motivated, from adding stickers to her calendar to represent the number of words written each day to creating a tiered reward system for larger word count milestones. Most recently, she writes each task she needs to complete on a sticky note, then adds the note to a jar once it's complete. "There's something that kicks in and gives a boost of dopamine [when] the project/writing goal is completed," she writes.

Consider organizing group writing or productivity sprints with friends, or set smaller goalposts for yourself to make it easier to keep track of forward progress. The National Novel Writing Month Wikipedia page, Wikiwrimo, provides a list of word crawls and other writing challenges authors can do on their own or alongside others: https://www.wikiwrimo.org/wiki/Word_crawl. Whether you use a dedicated platform or make your own rules, the reward is the same: making the road to your next published book just as fun as the finish line. ■

Nicole Schroeder

Nicole Schroeder

Nicole Schroeder is a storyteller at heart. As the editor in chief of Indie Author Magazine, she brings nearly a decade of journalism and editorial experience to the publication, delighting in any opportunity to tell true stories and help others do the same. She holds a bachelor's degree from the Missouri School of Journalism and minors in English and Spanish. Her previous work includes editorial roles at local publications, and she's helped edit and produce numerous fiction and nonfiction books, including a Holocaust survivor's memoir, alongside independent publishers. Her own creative writing has been published in national literary magazines. When she's not at her writing desk, Nicole is usually in the saddle, cuddling her guinea pigs, or spending time with family. She loves any excuse to talk about Marvel movies and considers National Novel Writing Month its own holiday.

From the Stacks

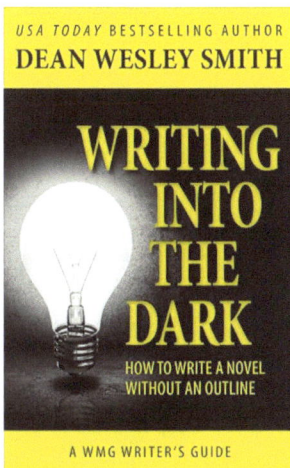

Writing into the Dark: How to Write a Novel without an Outline
Dean Wesley Smith
https://books2read.com/u/mdWq0l
Ask any pantser: you don't need an outline to write a best-selling novel. And *USA TODAY* best-selling author Dean Wesley Smith's book *Writing into the Dark* tells authors new to the drafting strategy how to do it. At only 118 pages, Smith's guide forgoes the fluff to share his strategy for finishing a first draft quickly, without plotting anything beforehand and with minimal editing required after. With advice intended to let your creative voice flourish and to maintain forward momentum, Smith's suggestions can be a fun craft exercise or a strategic plotting approach for authors to explore.

Brick
https://getbrick.app/shop
Plenty of virtual platforms incentivize authors to keep writing with rewards, progress bars, or timers, but if you find yourself especially prone to distraction, it may be worth exploring a physical tool to keep you on task. Brick is an app that pairs with a 3D-printed device to lock you out of specific apps and websites on your phone. Select the distractions you'd like to limit, tap your phone against the Brick to lock it, then again once you're ready to unlock it. Brick is currently only available for iPhone users, but developers are working on an Android-compatible version.

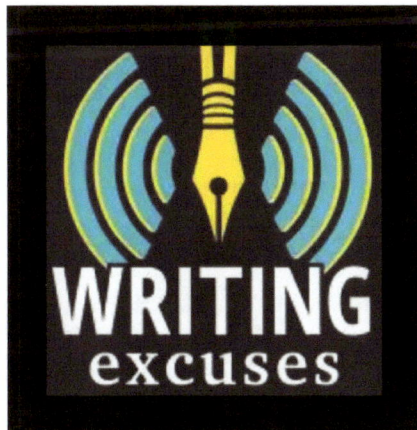

Writing Excuses
https://writingexcuses.com
Writing time is a precious commodity, but we'll consider the *Writing Excuses* podcast a valid distraction. Co-created by Howard Tayler, Dan Wells, and Brandon Sanderson, its fifteen-minute educational episodes focus mostly on craft, though they've also explored a variety of writing-adjacent topics such as dealing with burnout, managing finances, and understanding the public domain. Each episode also includes a homework assignment for you to put the lesson into practice. Currently hosted by five authors, the podcast is in its nineteenth season; Sanderson became a host emeritus in December 2022.

Indie Author Training Roundup

I f there's one thing we can be certain of in our indie author careers, it's that things change constantly, and trying to keep up can be a real time sink. Indie Author Training is a one-stop place that offers education, community, and tools for storytellers. New webinars, courses and product tours are coming online every week, and our discussion groups are always open for members to chat with one another, ask questions of thought leaders in the industry, and share tips without being subject to the whims of an algorithm.

In August, our series of webinars showcased Jeremy Flagg and Author Business Hub, a non-subscription productivity and workflow organization tool that can help you stay on track with every facet of your business. You can check out the replay here: https://indie-authortraining.com/webinars/author-business-hub.

We're finalizing the webinars for this coming month, so rush over to https://indieauthortraining.com/webinars to see what will help you in your career.

On the tech tools side, we've been busy releasing new product tours. These offer a quick whizz around a tool to show you its features firsthand and to help you decide if it would be useful for your indie author business. In August, we featured Merch Jar, an ads automation and management tool. If you want to see how to optimize the data from your Amazon ads in a useful way, Merch Jar can help. Check out how at https://indieauthortraining.com/merch-jar.

If you're looking for a specific training and we don't have it, drop into our suggestion group and let us know: https://indieauthortraining.com/groups/indie-author-training-courses-what-do-you-want-to-see. You can also suggest product tours and webinars. We'd love to hear from you!

Finally, if you want to receive regular updates on the live events we're hosting or join in on the fun in discussion groups, create an account at Indie Author Training for free at https://indieauthortraining.com. ■

Karen Guyler

AUTHOR BUSINESS HUB

With Jeremy Flagg

WATCH NOW

Does Your Academia Fiction Make the Grade across the Pond?

THE SIMILARITIES AND DIFFERENCES BETWEEN US AND UK SCHOOLS THAT MAY SHOW UP IN YOUR MANUSCRIPT

School is back in session, and for authors who write YA in academic settings, inspiration may be at the bus stop right outside your door. But if your story has dark academia tropes, light academia vibes, or a boarding school setting, you may need to brush up on the details of the student experience, especially if you are an American author writing about British characters. Here are a few ways the school systems differ, so you can meet reader expectations whether you write for fans of Harry Potter or *High School Musical*.

TYPES OF SCHOOLS

In the United States, most students attend public schools, which are funded by the government and free to attend. Students with means may attend private schools at varying levels of tuition. These schools are often run by a Catholic diocese but may also be founded by corporations or individuals and are sometimes affiliated with the military or a university. They are not subject to the same government mandates and standardized testing that public schools are. Magnet and charter schools have similar freedoms to private schools and are generally free to attend, but they may require testing for admittance.

The distinctions between British systems can be confusing for Americans. In England, the free, government-funded schools most students attend are referred to as "state schools." Ironically, fee-based schools are called "public" or "independent." Harrow and Eton, the school Prince William attended, are elite public schools.

GRADE LEVELS

American students typically begin formal schooling in kindergarten at age five, though they may attend preschool and other preparatory programs at three or four years old. After kindergarten, students progress from first through twelfth grade before graduation. Most schools are separated into elementary (kindergarten through grade five), middle (grades six through eight), and high (grades nine through twelve) schools, though in some areas, middle grades are rolled into either the elementary or high school. High school years are also referred to as freshman, sophomore, junior, and senior years, similar to at American college and university.

In England, students usually attend nursery school before their formal education begins with year 1 at age five. The last year of nursery school is referred to as reception. Years continue through year 13, when students graduate. Years 7 through 11, equivalent to American sixth to tenth grades, are called secondary school, which may surprise Americans, as that is the term used for American middle and high school years. British schools call the last two years "sixth form," or "college." These are the years Americans refer to as junior and senior year, or eleventh and twelfth grades.

Post-graduate schools in the UK are referred to exclusively as "university," or "uni." Americans may use the terms "college" and "university" interchangeably, but technically, American colleges are schools that focus on undergraduate programs (two- or four-year degrees). American universities usually offer a wider range of programs, including graduate and PhD levels, and may be composed of several associated colleges.

STUDENT EXPERIENCE

Beyond the overall structure of the school system in each country, students may encounter distinct school environments and cultures in the US and UK.

In the United States,

- at most free public schools, students do not wear uniforms.
- many students, especially in suburban or rural areas, ride a district school bus to and from school every day for free.
- students may form cliques based on common interests, though they are rarely as distinct as the jock, nerd, and band geek stereotypes found in media.
- schools tend to place high value on sports, like football, soccer, and basketball.
- schools typically give students ten to twelve weeks of vacation over the summer.

In England,

- students wear uniforms, usually consisting

of a blazer, sweater (jumper), dress shirt, and trousers or skirts. A tie is often required for every student, regardless of gender.

- students use public transportation or their parents' vehicles to get to school.
- students do not have the same stereotypes as in the US—partly because of their uniforms—but students tend to gravitate toward friends with common interests.
- schools do not have cheerleaders or marching bands. Rugby, cricket, and netball are popular sports. In general, school sports in the UK have lower stakes than they do in America, where scholarships are on the line.
- schools only get six weeks off for summer, but they have longer breaks during the year.

RESOURCES

To learn more about the differences between American and UK educational experiences, check out these personal accounts and one parent resource.

Teacher Tom of Eat Sleep Dream English discussed the differences between English and American schools in more detail with Jess Dante of Love and London on his YouTube channel.

Sunny in London has both a blog and a YouTube video that delve into the differences between US and UK schools from the perspective of an American mother who is married to an English man and whose children attend school in London.

American university students Noah Tang and Zack Maslanka student-taught in England in 2019. They discussed cultural differences in the classroom with Faith Ten Haken in an article for Illinois State University.

The Boarding School Review updated their comparison of UK and US educations in March 2024.

Although every school will have its own culture, and schools on both sides of the pond sometimes buck traditions, when writing about an academic setting, it's important to get the details right. Checking your facts can help your story earn top marks—that's high grades for Americans—and the reviews to match. ■

Jenn Lessmann

Jenn Lessmann

Jenn Lessmann is the author of Unmagical: a Witchy Mystery and three stories on Kindle Vella. A former barista, stage manager, and high school English teacher with advanced degrees from impressive colleges, she continues to drink excessive amounts of caffeine, stay up later than is absolutely necessary, and read three or four books at a time. Jenn is currently studying witchcraft and the craft of writing, and giggling internally whenever they intersect. She writes snarky paranormal fantasy for new adults whenever her dog will allow it.

Finding Light amid Dark Genres

HOW AUTHORS WRITING HEAVIER STORIES MANAGE THEIR MENTAL HEALTH

In the middle of research, author Terry Wells-Brown had to step away from her story. She'd interviewed a district attorney in charge of human trafficking for her book, but in the process of learning about the topic, it became too much to write about. She realized she needed to take a break before she could return to the page for her own well-being.

Writing means diving into your story, but writing a high-stakes story with dangerous situations, intense emotions, and dark themes can take an unexpectedly high toll on an author's mental health. When Elise Hoffman wrote intense scenes, like Wells-Brown, she also needed breaks to "recenter" herself, she said.

But it's not just the scenes and emotions themselves that can cause mental stress. Holding ourselves back from stories we want to tell can also be taxing. Joanna Penn, an author, podcaster, and business owner, identified this kind of pain in her book titled *Writing the Shadow*. Self-censorship and fear of judgment can hold authors back from tapping into the power of their darkness, she writes. Author Holly Roberds was concerned about writing a very dark story, but eventually she stopped worrying about how it would be received and just wrote it. "When I shed the judgment of what I was writing and allowed myself to follow the pull, I was SO joyful," she writes. "I needed to give myself permission to explore that space I wanted to explore. The real pain was judgment of what I wanted to express."

Although dark content can be difficult to write, filtering dark, intense, or scary elements of reality through a fiction lens is one way to sort through complex feelings. Authors Megan Linski and Dahlia T. Drake both identified current events as sources of stress that they could process as they wrote their books. Linski said, "My mental health is affected by the condition of the world, and processing that darkness needs to go somewhere, so I comprehend the world's problems by getting them out of me and onto the page."

The darker themes author K.G. Reuss includes in her books have also proved to be cathartic. "It's easy because I've personally been through it," Reuss said. "I can channel those memories and feelings and use them to drive the depth of the story. After I finish them, I feel satisfied because I know my FMC [female main character] is going to come out on top."

Although there is a lack of scientific research on the phenomenon, authors whose work has been weighing on them can identify an increase in general anxiety, restlessness, or malaise within themselves, as well as an avoidance of the darker writing. Others

report somatic symptoms, such as writing with a clenched jaw or tight shoulders. Friends or family members may also notice these changes. Whenever there are increased signs of stress, it's a sign that something needs to change, and noticing how you are feeling is a major way to monitor any impact dark content is having.

When the darkness weighs heavily, Hoffman will "watch a happy movie, read a fluffy romance, [or] watch cat videos" between writing intense scenes, she writes. Author Ivy Nelson does the same but finds that "keeping in mind how the scene … drives the plot or engages readers" in her book is also helpful. Kristen Gandy alternates writing lighter and darker books to maintain her equilibrium. Other stress relief techniques, such as walking in nature, exercise, therapy, or taking time away from the work can help authors cope with the stressors dark content can bring.

In the long term, however, continuing a certain series or genre may not always be worth the cost to your mental well-being. Author Meg Jolly said, "I had to quit a pen name because it was mentally tanking me." She loved the characters, but upon deciding to quit, she felt a wave of relief that told her it was the right decision.

Writing dark subjects can be rewarding as well as challenging. But paying attention to how you are feeling and listening to your gut can help you do it while maintaining your mental health. ◾

Jen B. Green

Jen B. Green

Jen B. Green has lived in five countries on four continents with her three sons, two daughters, and one great guy. She reads anything that stays still long enough, plays piano, and bakes everything sweet.

After earning her Ph.D. in psychology, Jen tried writing a novel for Nanowrimo and was hooked! Her days are spent traveling the world, teaching undergraduate psychology, and wrangling her growing homemade army, but her nights are for writing Urban Fantasy with witches and werewolves.

CLONE YOURSELF

Custom Chat GPT Bots

Harnessing AI's knowledge base and expand your skills and expertise in vital areas such as:

Life and Business Coaching
Mastering Marketing and Newsletter Strategies
Crafting Captivating Blurbs and Social Posts
Enhancing Time Management
Elevating Customer Service
Writing Compelling Ad, Product, and Landing Page Copy

And that's just the beginning.

INDIEAUTHORTRAINING.COM

www.ingramcontent.com/pod-product-compliance
Lightning Source LLC
Chambersburg PA
CBHW061141030426
42335CB00002B/63